FIERCE FAIRYTALES

FIERCE FAIRYTALES

& Other Stories to
Stir Your Soul

NIKITA GILL

First published in Great Britain in 2018 by Trapeze,
an imprint of The Orion Publishing Group Ltd
Carmelite House, 50 Victoria Embankment,
London EC4Y 0DZ

An Hachette UK company

10 9

A CIP catalogue record for this book is
available from the British Library.

ISBN (Hardback): 978 1 4091 8159 0
ISBN (ebook): 978 1 4091 8160 6

Printed and bound in Great Britain by Clays Ltd, Elcograf S.p.A.

www.orionbooks.co.uk

For you,
who has never forgotten
the magic.
It wants you to know
it remembers you too.

Contents

Contents

A Universal Truth

We all have storms and stories
inside our starmade bodies
that even the night sky cannot hold.

This is why we are on this earth;
to learn how to love each other,
to learn how to love and hold ourselves.

Once Upon A Time

Once upon a time,
Matter dreamed up an idea.

It was a small hopeful dream
a thought with the wings of the fairy.

But as with all things full of hope
it would be terribly difficult to birth.

Several events needed to come together
in the millisecond of the time it took to build Earth.

It depended on a 1 in $10^{2,685,000}$ chance of existing.
A 1 in 20,000 chance meeting between two beings.

An ancestral heritage that goes back 4 billion years
all the way to single-celled organisms.

And only then can this idea be so finely crafted
into a gift with actual presence.

Imagine how much the universe must have loved
this thing to make it happen.

Imagine how many stars gave up their hearts
to bring this into fluid motion.

Does it make you curious?
Make you wonder what could be so marvellous?

That idea . . . it was you.
You are the universe's fairytale come true.

Once Upon A Time II

But the universe never promised
you this would be easy,
after all, you are the hero here.

And heroes are meant
to be forged golden
from the blaze.

It is up to you to rise again
from the fragmented shards
your foes left of you.

You must lift a sword
with reborn strength and take on
the demons in your ribcage.

You must devastate the chains
every violent person
has brutally placed on you.

And you must show them all
how *they* were simply
characters in *your* story.

But you, you are the author
of this spellbinding tale
built of hope and bravery.

Out there may be monsters, my dear.
But in you still lives the dragon
you should always believe in.

For the Cynic

Our current cosmic address
is a small flying piece of rubble
travelling through an endless black void,
surrounded inexplicably
by seven other pieces of flying rubble.

All of these pieces harmoniously
rotate around the same giant fireball
without ever crashing into each other
or hurtling themselves
into said fireball.

And if that isn't random enough,
out of all those pieces of rubble
ours is the only one that sustains
an environment that gives life
to billions of different life forms,

including a multitude
of flowering plants
and oxygen-giving trees,
a plethora of wildlife
and eight billion human beings.

And somehow,
you still
genuinely think
that magic does not exist,
that fairytales aren't real,

that the way people
find each other
at just the right time
at just the right moment
isn't the most powerful sorcery.

Somewhere Across the Universe, This Intergalactic Fairytale is Being Told

In the far corner of the Virgo supercluster, a small galaxy called the Milky Way exists, and in one of the further spirals of that galaxy there is said to be a tiny planet called Earth. At a cursory glance, there is nothing seemingly unique about this planet, even though it is simply beautiful, cloaked in calypso blue with an oscillating belt of green. It is, in fact, one of millions like it that live in just this universe.

The extraordinary thing about this planet, though, is the beings that exist on it. They have been through war after war. Empires that promised to burn brighter than their resident star, the sun, and disappeared in the blink of an eye. Savage rulers, dictators have destroyed entire portions of it, and yet . . . they simply refuse to stop existing, it is like they have this treasured thing within them to keep them surviving, and to keep knowing.

Look closer now, oh passer-by, look closer at these beings. They are survivors with a sense of awe and curiosity at everything around them. Sometimes they have lost their way, but this is a thing they never seem to lose, because they are so full of potential.

Promise. This planet may be called Earth, but it should have been called Promise.

If you do not believe this little story, and dismiss it as a silly old wives' tale, a thing which cannot possibly exist, then I hope you come upon their legendary message. You see, 40 years ago, these beings sent out a message on a space probe that has travelled 20.5 billion kilometres, hoping to meet one of us in space. In it lies a message, the definition of this entire species, and it reads simply:

'This is a present from a small distant world, a token of our sounds, our science, our images, our music, our thoughts, and our feelings. We are attempting to survive our time so we may live into yours.'

The Voyager is still out there, waiting for someone to come upon it. Maybe that someone is you. Maybe you will remind that species of the greatness that lies in their potential, their promise. Maybe you will be the being that helps turn that fairytale planet of promise into an intergalactic legend of green and blue.

A Tale of Two Sisters

In the beginning, there was oblivion.
A vastness, and an abyss comprised
of darkness and nothingness,
 ... until there were two sisters.

One was made from the interconnectedness
of all things, a precipice of stories,
a treasury of things gone and things to come.
Her name was Cosmos.

The other was made from the tricorn
of darkness: black magic waiting to be born,
inkwells of feral power and rebel thoughts.
Her name was Chaos.

Before they had floated into the abyss,
as all celestial beings were left to do in the end,
their father told them to be a binary system,
to never ever let go of each other.

He warned them that together they could
build everything, but apart, nothing could exist.
So the two came together and imagined a tapestry
of moving, living stars that inhaled around each other.

They pictured impossible things like planets
that help thousands of different beings
and balls of fire to keep them warm
and whole atmospheres to help them breathe.

And this was how the love of two sisters
wrote the first ever eternal poem into magical
loving existence. A single poem
they christened, 'The Uni-verse'.

The Fable in Thermodynamics

The first law of thermodynamics states this:
'energy can neither be created nor destroyed.'

Which is to say everything around us is recycled energy,
you, me, your dog, those we love and those we avoid.

Which is to say that the energy that makes us
is as ancient as the beginning of time itself.

Which is to say that our bones could have been
fragmented together from the ashes of the library of
    Alexandria.

Which is to say our sinews and spine were crafted from the
end of a hundred-year-old oak tree and our smiles a comet.

Which is to say our hearts could be Achilles' spirit
when he battled at Troy, bringing his enemies down with it.

Which is to say, when we feel like life is overwhelming,
we must remember that we're just sparks of energy borrowing
    skin.

That no matter how much this pain feels everlasting,
this is just the temporary fabric we are in.

The Woods Reincarnated

We traded the woods for high-rises,
the wolf became the boy next door,
soft brown eyes and close-lipped smiles
to hide the flash of fangs instead of teeth.
The huntsman became the 'nice' man
that happened to live down the street
whose laugh never quite reached his eyes,
and the beaten track gets hazy
between grandmother and beast.
I wonder where the wildest things go
when the devilled copse is no longer there.
When the forest paths
become the backstreets of a city,
where predators learn a sweeter language
accented with false niceties.
The stories where little girls
need to be street-smart to survive
and sometimes they don't win,
sometimes it's the wolf that thrives.
What happens to the fairytale
when the woods have been replaced by cities;
and a concrete jungle that comes to life?

Whispers from the Wicked Woods

Where are the stories for the wicked girls,
the ones where they are told perfection is a lie?

Where are the legends fashioned from nuance,
the ones that cause the hero and the villain to blur lines?

Where are the myths for darker things,
the ones of us who were never snow-white pure?

Where are the lessons for naughty children,
the ones who want to be lost in the forest and folklore?

If you're looking for secrets you will find them here,
these words have been resurrected from old fairytales' ruins.

This is the place where those stories come to be reborn
and from the wreckage emerge things
more human than humans.

The Miller's Daughter

The queen addresses her firstborn
after the fall of Rumpelstiltskin:

Maybe magic ends with me
and it will never cross your path
but I want you to remember
that survival is an art.
The world is falsehood
so you rely on your smarts.

Princes fail all the time.
Passion sometimes goes cold.
And princesses on days of fortune
can turn straw into gold.
Kind kings become greedy
and dragons can have soft souls.

Fairies cast the wrong spells,
mermaids can be drowned,
goblins and trolls can be heroes
and giants can fall without a sound,
and even the darkest things can be defeated
once their names are spoken out loud.

Half of Rumpelstiltskin Seeks Redemption

Half of Rumpelstiltskin
speaks to the Miller's Daughter:

Since tearing myself in two,
the half of me that remains
has been learning how to grow
and craft an apology worthy of you.

I offer no tricks, only regret
for not understanding in my childhood
that guilt is sometimes necessary,
a way to remember good and never forget.

I have heard that excuses make
for bad apologies, so I'll stop there.
All I want to say is this: I am sorry
but I do not say it for forgiveness' sake.

There are no asterisks here.
Your feelings are completely valid,
you are under no obligation to pardon me,
I have yet to earn it for putting you through fear.

What I am trying to say is,
I know now that becoming kind
is worth every single exhausting effort
and sometimes it takes a thousand years.

Today, I apologised to someone
I owe an ocean full of amends to.
Tomorrow, I will teach myself
the kindness alphabet from scratch.

If this is not what an apology looks like,
if this is not what *growth* looks like,
I do not know what they are.

Why Tinkerbell Quit Anger Management

I had to give up on their remedies.
They kept trying to make me less angry,
but I refuse to surrender my rage.

Because whole kingdoms have already spent
millennia trying to keep women subdued,
only to be discarded in old age.

My fury gets things done,
it has saved lives, it has made the world listen;
where I could not speak, my anger has screamed.

Think Helen of Troy when they took her freedom.
Think the Rani of Jhansi leading rebellions.
Think Joan of Arc leading armies on what she dreamed.

So now I love my tinderbox heart
so easy to light up,
all it takes is half a spark.

A woman's anger can change the world,
I know mine can and this is not a gift
I will give away.

I am small and I am angry,
it is how I channel my energy
and I *like* me that way.

Boy Lost

Picture a sunset in a small port town by the sea. Two teenaged boys sitting on the docks watching the ships as they fly across the water. One reaches out and takes the other's hand. In this brush of skin on skin, a thousand unspoken promises erupt between them, and both are determined to keep them. This is what youth is. The sheer belief that you will be able to keep every promise you made to someone else. That you will be able to love someone into a forever when you do not even understand what forever means.

An evening spent in the headiness of love, they go back to their respective homes. One boy helps his mother with cooking and cleaning and looking after his little sister. His father is a good man, a sailor who brings home with him meagre wages but a heart full of love and a quicksilver tongue that tells stories of faraway lands to enthral them all. But this boy, despite his blessings, is not happy. He may have been blessed with a loving family, but that faraway look is made of unrest and wanderlust; something about him says fae, changeling, wearing the skin of a boy who was always destined to fly, to leave.

The other boy returns home to a father who drinks and a mother who works so hard that she is never there. He is the unwanted creature in this home, a beating waiting for him at every corner. His father's temper is a beast so powerful that a boy made of paper bones barely held together cannot fight him. He hides in his room. He lives for a boy at sunset, hope made into a human being.

Now picture this. This boy of paper bones alone at the docks the next sunset. And this boy alone on the docks again on a rainy day. And this boy alone on the docks every day after, waiting for someone who promised him forevers he never

intended to keep. This boy becoming a man, a heart wounded so young in youth that it never quite healed right. Imagine him becoming a sailor, searching land after land for a boy he once loved, thinking he was hurt, or stolen, just needing to know what happened to him.

Now see him finally finding out that the boy he loved in his boyhood ran away to a magical land where he never grew up. That, without a second glance, he just forgot every promise of forever. Imagine his rage, that ancient pain turning to a terrible anger and escaping from the forgotten attic of his mangled heart. Think of what happens when immense love turns into immense hate. An anger so intense it cannot be controlled. What he would give up to avenge the boy he once was, paper-boned, standing on the docks, broken, without a single person to love him, simply all alone. A hand is a small price to pay for a magical ship that will take him to Neverland, a place that lives on a star. Becoming a villain called Captain Hook is a small exchange to show Peter Pan that you cannot throw away love and think you will get away unscarred.

Wendy

No one talks about what happened to Wendy Darling after they returned from Neverland. No one speaks of Wendy Darling anymore. The truth is, whilst her parents were able to convince her brothers that Neverland never happened, that all children must grow up, that it was all just a dream, Wendy knew better and she vehemently believed.

She believed when her friends made fun of her in boarding school. She wished for the fairies to save her when she went to the headteacher's office and her parents were forced to remove her. She even spoke to Peter after that when she was home-schooled by her governess. As she grew older, the visions of Neverland never quite ceased and she painted and drew pictures showing her wonderful adventures with Peter and the Lost Boys. She didn't realise her parents were slowly growing concerned and wrung their hands about how she would ever find a man to marry, if she still believed in all this nonsense.

Things came to a head when Wendy refused to marry. Soon they grew so worried that they had Wendy placed in an asylum, claiming her hallucinations were so terrible that they needed tending. You would think the story would end there, but Wendy had a powerful faith in herself and in the strength of her own mind and memory.

So from the asylum she began to write stories and paint pictures of Neverland for children, impressing everyone, soothing the patients to the point that her doctor, a kind-hearted man, began to send her work to publishers. Wendy, slowly but surely, became so adamant and so polite to her doctors that they began to question their own sanity, because she remained so unfalteringly faithful to her story. However, if she had no means of supporting herself, she would never be able to leave this asylum, and knowing this was going to be her fate, Wendy once again wished upon the fairies.

They had never paid her any mind before, but her fervour made them pay attention. Because they guided her to send her writings and paintings to a publisher who absolutely loved what she was doing. They offered her enough money to leave the asylum, which she could when she turned 21, and support herself; something almost unheard of in their circle of society.

Wendy died a happy old maid, with a dozen books she had written, a stunning library and a host of friends and nephews and nieces that absolutely loved and thought the world of her.

But this is the reason why no one talks of Wendy Darling anymore. Because the most successful children's books of her time, the adventures in Neverland, were never published under the name of Wendy Darling, but simply under 'Wendy'.

Child's Play

It always begins when we are children
with imaginations so big we put
whole universes to shame.

Whilst running and playing
and shouting in the white-hot sun
before prejudices stop our feet.

We tell each other stories
layered with childlike epiphany
and fiery self-belief.

We squabble over who
gets to play the princess
or the hero prince.

None of us want to be
the dragon that is slayed
nor the ogre nor the witch.

Right there in our child's mind
we decide everyone can
only be very evil or very good.

We never stop to consider
that all of us are capable
of doing terrible things.

But if we look back
and we try to truly understand
we will remember what we should.

We have all taken turns
being Red Riding Hood
and we have all been the wolf.

The Red Wolf

Children go missing all the time.
Sometimes it is faeries who steal them.
Other times, they trust a wolf.

Even in times of war, children are innocent to the true ways of the world. Their mothers are always wiser.

This is because most mothers know that the softest people with the biggest hearts are the ones who held the truest magic of them all; purity of this kind could not be bought from the Gods themselves, and it was the greatest target of the devil-souled.

When Little Red Riding Hood went missing, a girl so beloved by her mother that she always told her she could be *anything* she wanted to be, her mother never ever left the place where she had grown up, hoping against hope that the trees, the woods, would one day return her child.

Every day, she stood at the edge of the woods, looking into the dark, hoping to find a wisp of her forest-hearted child somewhere within the leaf-strewn wild. Every day, she took a step closer to the darkness, hopelessness making her courage steadfast, stronger.

Grief makes unlikely warriors out of us all.

So when she saw the two lamp-like eyes in the dark one day, she was not afraid. Instead she asked, 'Brother wolf, are you the one who has stolen my child from my arms and taken her away?'

'Not I,' said the wolf before disappearing.

The next day, she took another step closer to the woods she had

once searched every inch of and another pair of eyes glowed through the darkness, red like the colour of her child's cloak.

'Brother wolf, are you the one who pulled my child away from me with just a look?'

'Not I,' said the red-eyed wolf before turning away.

A wolf began to visit her almost every day. And every day she would ask the same question a different way. She found herself getting closer and closer to the heart of the forest and the wolves never ever attacked her. She began to wonder if what the woodcutter had told her was true, that a wolf had eaten her child for its supper.

On the day she reached the heart of the forest, she began to realise that although she had *thought* she had been here before, this lush, dense part of the woods was a place she had never been. There was something both familiar and unsettling about it, almost like a place not meant to be seen.

A lair where a thousand lamp-like eyes watched her from the fog and the dark, and when the fog cleared away and the light came through, she found what she was looking at was enough to make her fall apart. On a throne amongst wolves of all sorts and sizes, a young girl sat. She wore a red wolf's skin on her body and two swords sheathed behind her back.

Slow recognition crept over her face. She ran to the older woman and, after hugging her, finally told her why she had never come home.

'Dear Mother, I am sorry I never ever came home. The evil woodcutter and his friends were trying to destroy this forest world. When I came through the woods, I happened to hear of all of their plans. They saw me listening, followed me to grandmother's, killed her and tried to burn her house down with me in it so they could continue their wicked plans. The wolves came to rescue me, and trained me to be one of them. I am now the Alpha and protect them from the woodcutter and his evil friends.'

Her mother promised her that she would never tell another soul where Red Riding Hood was. The secrecy was their only weapon against the woodcutter and his horde. Over and over again, Red Riding Hood and the wolves bravely defended the woods and woodland creatures from extinction. They bravely fought and her mother soon came to live with them and aid them in their battle.

So when you tell the story of Red Riding Hood, remember this too:

Her mother told her
she could grow up to be
anything she wanted to be,
so she grew up to become
the strongest of the strong,
the strangest of the strange,
the wildest of the wild,
the wolf leading the wolves.

Cinderella's Mother Sends Her a Message from Heaven

When you were just a little girl, I told you to have courage and to be kind, and that is how I will be with you throughout your life.

You were so small and so sweet when I left you alone in this world. It hurt you so much that you took those words, gently wrapped them in one of my silk handkerchiefs, slept with them under your pillow every night.

When your papa brought a new mama home for you, you tried, you really tried. You cooked and you cleaned, wore your little body into cinders and bloodwork for her and her daughters, who spoke about you like you were never there, even when you were fixing their corsets, mending their dresses, helping them dress. Not a word of thanks fell from their lips. They sent you as far away as they could, to the attic, but you made the best of their cruelty, didn't you, my sweet girl? You slept on a nest you made from tattered clothes and hay, befriended the mice up there, shared your meagre food with them instead of keeping them at bay.

Darling, some people wear the word 'family' as a disguise for their intentions and who they are. Darling, I should have taught you this, should have reminded you of what you are. I should have told you, be kind, but remember kindness does not mean being covered in soot, and used, and laughed at, and forgotten. I should have taught you courage meant standing up for yourself and what self-worth truly means.

You do not need to wait for permission, no one will think less of you when you decide to take back what has always been rightfully yours. No one deserves the right to steal from the garden of your heart that you so lovingly grew, and swallowing your own pride should not be one of your chores. Let no one tell you that kindness and courage can only wear the skin of giving up your self-worth, that you cannot wear your self-respect like it is armour. Stand up for your own human dignity and roar.

The Stepmother's Tale

People are going to betray you the way
Judas betrayed Jesus,
the way Brutus betrayed Caesar,
and you will love them anyway.

And betrayal comes
in so many different shapes and forms.
No one ever tells you
how death too
is a form of betrayal.

How life too betrays you
by robbing you of the person
you depend on, your soulmate.

She didn't start that way. None of us are truly born evil. Evil is man-made. Once, she was a beautiful young girl who grew up working in her father's flour mill; a good daughter with a light heart, as girls were expected to be during that time, and she never complained, no matter how hard or burdensome the work was.

When she turned 18, she began to accompany her father to the market to sell the flour they made, and a rich merchant saw her, this lovely, hard-working young woman with an easy smile. Unlike most men of his time, he was progressive. Instead of asking her father's permission immediately to marry her, he asked permission from her first, and then her father if he could court her. He wasn't handsome, but he had a soft look about his eyes and gentle hands, and it was long into their courtship that she fell in love with him. They married and had two little daughters, and, as fairytales like this go, should have had a happily ever after.

But life instead had a tale of woe in plan for this woman and her girls.

Soon after the seventh birthday of her second daughter, her husband took ill and died. And whilst grieving for the man she loved, she learned how unkind the world is to a single mother of daughters. Where she once had plenty of comfort to live in and provide her children with, soon the debt collectors started appearing at every hour and a quarter. She looked for work but found nothing suitable for the mother of two small children. Months faded to years and slowly they grew more and more destitute until she did the only thing she could do in dark desperation. She found another man, one she did not love, but who was grieving his lost love too, and married him, promising to give his orphaned child a mother.

Desperation turns people sour, and she now saw life as an open wound. A shallow promise. A dark thing that should have loved her but instead tried to drown her. Her beauty fading, she recognised that she had failed to pass on her looks to her two daughters. And now she knew how important it is for a woman to be beautiful, as it is the only currency she truly has in this world, she became even more bitter. So when she saw Cinderella and her goodness and her beauty, all she could think is, *That used to be me.* And the more she saw the kindness that was in Cinderella, the more she wanted to take it from her, so Cinderella would understand how awful life can be.

She is cruel to Cinderella because she wants to teach her, in her own terrible, misguided way, that,

'Life is not going to be kind
just because you are pretty,
and yet your beauty
is your only true currency.

If I can just teach you how to be
cautious and cruel instead
of so naive and kind,
I can stop you from
becoming yet another me.'

Lessons in Surviving Long-term Abuse

She listened to the roar of the thunderstorm,
She fell in love with the fragrance of petrichor,
She searched the night sky for shooting stars,
She planted flowers on her meagre windowsill
to brighten up her attic room every evening.
She hid away books with words that would
touch her slowly fraying soul,
She took pleasure in the smell of fresh-baked
bread that she had just brought out of the oven.
She made friends with all the mice who lived inside
and all of the birds who nested outside
in little pots and shoeboxes
she had given them to reside in.

She placed her trust in these little things
to keep her alive,
and this was how Cinderella survived.

Fairy Godmother

For years, I was a closed gate.
Prayers escaped my lips, affirmations
in two different languages.

Ask me what I was praying for,
and I will tell you; a Fairy Godmother
who never appeared for me.

But that is what faith is, I was told.
Finding a reason to believe even when
no reason finds its way to you.

So I began to find her in odd places.
That time the car narrowly missed me.
That time the sea nearly drowned me but couldn't.

That time when I thought I had found a tragic ending
but instead ended up finding a beginning
dipped in peace and all things holy.

I used to think that prayer would solve everything.
I still believe that firmly. Except the prayers
that I utter now are stronger in what they believe.

You see, at the end, I learned the truth about her.
My Fairy Godmother lives in the details.
My Fairy Godmother is my heart sustaining me.

Two Misunderstood Stepsisters

If you ever want to have
a look at the way a word
can totally demean and destroy
the entire worth and value of a woman,
just look at what the word 'ugly'
did to Cinderella's two stepsisters.

Children aren't born abusive, it is nurtured in them. Children aren't born ugly either. They learn to hate themselves from society's narrow-minded ideas about how they must feel unsatisfied in their own skin.

Let me start at the beginning of this tale, one filled with considerable pain for all involved.

These two sisters may have seemed fortunate because they had pretty dresses and nice things, but they also had the misfortune of growing up as the not-so-pretty daughters of one of the most beautiful women in the world, a burden that they bore on their little bones till their bodies had no choice but to grow fangs. This is what real damage looks like: a sweet, innocent little girl being told over and over again how ugly she is until it becomes a storm raining down on her innocence, forcing her to choose cruelty over kindness.

You can give her a million lovely things in the form of silks and necklaces and diamonds, but through your cruel words, you are still killing the thing which is most valuable inside her, the softness inside her soul.

This is also what the human instinct to survive looks like; you become the thing that hurts you until it can hurt you no more.

First and foremost, girls are survivors. We are trained to expect the world to be toxic to us and make the best of a bad situation by developing the skills to survive it. No one ever says the skills won't be toxic. No one ever mentions how we are cruel sometimes and we don't choose it.

So when they see Cinderella, a girl who bears both the envied beauty they have been tormented about, as well as an innocence they were robbed of, they take out their rage on her. This is what happens when girls are taught other girls are competition instead of their sisters. This is what happens when we make women think their outer beauty is all that matters.

We end up stealing from them their hearts, their souls, their softness, by making them believe that none of that really matters.

This is what I mean when I say:

If all girls were taught
how to love each other fiercely
instead of how to compete
with each other
and hate their own bodies,
what a different and beautiful world
we would live in.

Trapped

You may be gentle and sad now, girl,
but you are still made from daring dreams,
wade through the silhouetted thoughts in your
own hapless mind that harness you.

He is mercurial with his love
but more so his violence.

Knowing this need not be a ruinous thing.
Knowledge after all is a dark art,
full to the brim with liberty,
a trembling, malleable power.

And it is yours for the taking.

You were called Alice
after your mother, who took on
jabberwocks and armies and won.
Your own jabberwock awaits.

Fearless already runs through your blood.
Now do it justice.

Badroulbadour

Her father gave her a name
near impossible to pronounce
but every refugee child's
tongue says it
as easily as a prayer.

She once lived in a palace,
now she lives in a war zone.
Her fairytale ended the day
the first bomb dropped,
and the first child died.

Her city is no longer a city,
even though it is still home,
littered with the bodies
of what once were her people,
who now by missile Medusa's wrath are stone.

The once princess now
wanders the bloodied streets,
trying to help orphans,
and giving the injured
food and water.

What a far cry this is
from the mystical tale
of a boy with a lamp;
there are no more genies, they met
a different kind of metallic murder.

There is no magic carpet
to save the wounded.
Just Badroulbadour,
princess turned paramedic,
the Sultan's brave and only daughter.

The Shoemaker's Son

Baba told him one night
when the desert storm rose high,
Poor men's sons do poor men's jobs.

This is just their destiny.
They have no right to dreams.
No right to build sky palaces.

No right to pursue silly ideas
like magic and sorcery,
or flirting with alchemy.

Yet something ancient in the boy's heart
did not allow him to give up the fact
that a bigger destiny ran in his arteries.

Baba would die a shoemaker,
in his little stand at the market
behind which they slept at night.

And the boy would be left orphaned,
having lost his mother young,
and not an uncle or aunt in sight.

But do not despair for this child,
for he is made of fight and flames
and an intrinsic need for learning.

He pleads with the palace guards
to let him be an errand boy and slowly
makes his way through his own scheming.

Winning everyone's trust, he meets a physician
who teaches him everything that you can possibly
do with a royal apothecary.

Steadily, he understands chemical magic
by romancing his way through atom theories,
almost-enchanted potions and his careful study.

Baba was wrong; even poor men's
children can, through their own cunning,
construct entirely different destinies.

Who would have thought that a mere
shoemaker's son would go on to become
Ja'far the Sultan's most trusted vizier.

Scheherazade the Clever

A clever woman is more lethal
than a freshly crafted magic wand,
and this is why she is feared.
She is unpredictable, and unpredictable
is another word for 'threat'
when a woman wears it well.
This is why they try
to snatch her power away.
Vilify her by saying she is
dangerous, manipulative, insane.
Whip 'no' and the fight out of
their daughters early
so they don't turn out like her.
The vixen, the vamp, the witch;
they have so many words
to convey their dislike of this woman,
because she holds her own
on a planet clearly not built
for humans like her.

But how else is a woman supposed to survive
if not by her wits?
Look at the tale of the Sultan Shahryar,
whose fragile masculinity
punished a thousand innocent women
by marrying them and then
murdering them the next day
for a single act of unfaithfulness
committed by his wife,
and no one could stop the strife
being rained down on the women of the kingdom.
Until he met his match in a girl armed

with nothing but her wits and a thousand stories,
one for every girl he killed.

Imagine this girl, Scheherazade,
visiting the dead lake where the bodies
were drowned, speaking with the women
like they were her sisters,
'It ends with me, I promise you,
it ends with me.'

And no other girl
was ever harmed after she told Shahryar
her never-ending story,
full of the spirit tales of the women
he so mercilessly murdered,
until he couldn't help but be
entranced by her spell.
Open sesame,
a girl becomes a queen.
Open sesame,
a vizier's daughter outwits a king.
Open sesame,
a crafty woman is stronger
than a band of forty powerful thieves.
Open sesame.
This is the oldest kind of witchcraft
that has ever lived and never leaves.
Open sesame. Open sesame. Open sesame.

Wonderland Villain

Yes, I am dreadful
and I am desolate
and I am difficult to digest

No, I do not apologise
for the things that I am
for what makes me today

I am that dark thing
that you loved to hate
now the terror that keeps you awake

Call me gross
Call me stupid
Call me disgusting

None of those names
can ever hurt me again
I am a thousand treacherous things

I was not made
to be lovely for you
I was made to eat monsters for ME

I never lied
I never claimed not to make mistakes
I never said I was a saint

When you bullied
me with those names as a child
you made a horrible mistake

This is not silence
you saw in response to you
that was me putting on war paint

You can hate me for it
but I am both nightmare and sin
I wear thunder underneath this skin

I am both storm and calm
I am queen of all the hearts I consume
you made me this thing that you do not like

Now nothing will save you
when you look into the mirror
when you try to sleep at night

The Hatter

To understand what they did to the Hatter, I must first tell you about people who know how to play with your brokenness like it is a fidget spinner without so much as touching your skin – a form of abuse known as gaslighting.

You say it happened, they say it did not.

You say it has to, they say it cannot.

They pull at a thread of pain left by someone in your mind, and sew an entire ghost out of you.

Build you a dark wonderland and ask you to call it home. Tell you, 'Why can't you just be happy.' And you cannot, because happiness in this story is a queen you do not trust being built from your own delusions.

When this happens, you are like the Hatter. Trapped here in this fairytale world, half mad because someone you love keeps lying to you.

Is this rain, dear? *No it isn't, it's a raven.*

Is this a door? *No, it is a writing desk.*

Is this my mind? *No, it is now my rabbit hole, and I'm going to make you fall so far down there is no way out.*

This is why the raven becomes like a writing desk, nonsensical riddles and memories become valid, nothing makes sense anymore anyway.

You start wondering if anything you ever thought happened to you actually happened to you and *this* is their violence. This is their abuse. It has left bruises and gashes along your brain that no one else knows are there.

Doubting yourself is now a reflex. Trusting yourself is no longer muscle memory but a long, strenuous process.

They called the Hatter
completely mad.
Because he is cursed
to both remember
and to forget.

They call me mad too
because my curse is to heal
through remembering
everything you tried
to make me forget.

How a Hero Becomes a Villain

Trauma when left untreated
has the capacity to make
a villain out of you.

No one understands how little boys
who save villages, who become war heroes,
who have fathers that just expect
them to be brave no matter the cost
to the insides of their minds, become
villains without even trying to.

How then hearing the word 'no' becomes a trigger,
how love rejected becomes
cautiously pieced self-worth dissolved,
how the thought of losing love and it being
given to someone else makes this
entire facade you have carefully constructed fall.

How you weren't always an arrogant,
self-involved, obsessive bad guy, how that is
just the way you project yourself
to keep the vulnerable little boy hidden,
this is what is expected of you,
the strongest man in the whole village.

How obsession is a symptom of a dark
thing left untreated, and how truthfully
under your brash surface you have kept a beast
inside you secretly hidden, and what seeing the girl you love
hand over her love to someone who looks
just like the demon you fight every night does.

This is how a hero like Gaston
becomes the devil in the story which could
have been about his only chance at finding love.

Take this as your reminder.
Not all heroes wear capes.
Some wear darkness, some wear wounds.

Beauty and Bravery

I'll tell you a secret no one
wants you to know.

You do not have to be good to be brave.
You do not have to be perfect,
your mind completely clear,
your heart full of joy,
everything soft and sacred.

They make it out like the brave never lie, but the truth is, all of us lie at least twice a day and that has no bearing on how much courage you can hold in your heart.

When I set out to save my father, I was not being brave. I was acting out of fear of losing the only parent I ever had. They may want you to believe that I was simply being brave, but anxiety makes more heroes than history would care to repeat, it is better than sitting and waiting, letting the demon claw into your mind with worry. Anxious people are resourceful, they need to know how to keep the sea of panic at bay so they do not drown.

When I chose to stay at the palace in place of my father, I was not being brave. I was acting out of love. The idea of him here, sick, old, in this damp prison, under the care of that beastly creature when I, healthy, young, could take his place, of course I chose to take his place, what would you do? We would all give up even the ashes of ourselves for a parent we love more than this fire of a life.

When I chose to come back for the beast, I was not being brave. I was acting out of devotion and panic at the idea of loss. This being, who had respected my love of books, who was the only one who had ever known the real me and esteemed me for who I am, I came back for him, I could not let them take him *from me*. We do not abandon those who truly accept us for who we are, and if you could save all the people who accepted you completely, wouldn't you go back to save them too?

So I'll tell you a secret
no one wants you to know.

You do not have to be good to be brave.
You just need to know how to love.
You just need to unfold your heart
and recognise where you stand
and who you are.

Cry Wolf

They wrote the story wrong,
the boy was crying wolf, it's true,
but he didn't need a saviour.
He was warning them
about what the wolf *in him*
was about to do.

Jack's Fable Unfalsified

Everyone in this world
is in the habit of letting
everyone else down.

We write songs about it
and poetry and sweet stories,
but people hurting each other

will never become pretty.
Every time a heart breaks
and repairs, there are scars.

This is why they call it
heartbreak not just sadness.
To encapsulate the full extent

of the shatter.

Jack's mother chose the bottle over him every time. And every time she did, she explained it this way, 'You need to learn to be more self-absorbed, child. Who else will look out for you if you do not look out for yourself?' And he used this as an excuse for his mother's cruelty towards him. This was the thing he bit down on when her hatred of his father rained down on him instead. When the bottle spoke through her fists. When she forgot how little he was. When he heard the neighbours quietly speak, clucking their tongues, 'Poor child, imagine having to live with *that*,' and he knew they weren't wrong.

Children with abusive, alcoholic parents learn excuses and lies to survive. They learn the value of a good lie being the difference between stability and a beating. When you are small enough, your brain works quicker to learn how to keep you alive, and forgiving his mother her harshness became a thing he did for himself, to save his own mind from realising this was hell.

She wasn't able to stop him from being kind, though. He got his kindness from his father, and his father never failed to remind him when he was smaller, 'Son, millions of people die every year, but you are still here and this is because you are doing something right.'

So Jack learned to focus. He thought of the hard-working old farm woman he passed every day on his way to school, who never stopped to wave at him, even though it probably hurt her to do so. He thought of her two tiny grandchildren who had lost their parents too young.

But then his father also said, 'I'm sorry, I don't know how I can help you with why your mother is the way she is. Just know this, she loves you, no matter what you think, okay?' And when the parent who doesn't hit you backs up the parent that does, that just adds to the layer of betrayal that is already grafting over your heart. This is a fresh wound now.

So Jack tried not to pick at it. Instead he fixated on how happy the old woman he saw every day was, how happy her two grandchildren were, even though they had nothing.

His father died after a brief battle with illness. His mother never stopped cursing him as weak. Given his father's inability to stand up to her, he couldn't bring himself to disagree there either. So instead he began to work on himself. He looked at both his parents and thought, I *shall take the best parts of you and make a new me from them*. This was how Jack became kind and he became strong. That day when his mother gave him the old cow to sell, he practised both these qualities.

He gave the cow to the old farm woman. At the very least, she could give her grandchildren milk. On her insistence, he took what she called magic beans, although he thought they were just the product of someone tricking this naive, hard-working old soul. He took them home to his mother and, for the first time in his entire life, he stood his ground. And the storm came, a violent swell, several blows, the beans taken from him and chucked out the window.

But it wasn't about the beans. It never was. It was about being better than both his parents. It was about not tiptoeing around who he was to please someone else. It was about turning from victim to survivor.

The beanstalk wasn't the story really.

The abuse always was.

Jack was never foolish.
He just climbed the beanstalk
to get away from his personal demons.

Jack was never silly.
He would rather face giants
than the tragedy of a vicious parent.

Goldilocks

This is what Goldilocks learned
from the bears that day
in the woods by taking
and breaking things
that were not hers;

so many places, people,
and borrowed infinities
we pretend are ours,
all for a snatched second
of happiness,

only to break everyone
and everything
we have ever loved
and watch it all
disappear into the ether.

The Three Times You Rebuilt Your House-shaped Heart

The first time your house-shaped
heart is wrecked
you are too young to realise
love can be a wolf.

They call it puppy love
but there is something
deeply violent in this,
too violent to be that innocent.

Slowly, you rebuild it.
With confidence
you make it out of straw,
sturdier than no protection.

And again, it is wrecked.
Huffed and puffed into nothingness
by this dangerous thing
no one wants to call a wolf.

Again, you collect
from the wreckage,
promise yourself stronger,
make a wooden shelter.

But even this proves
futile, for the dark thing
that relishes destroying
your soft, wanting heart.

It takes you so much longer
to feel and trust again,
you build walls made of brick.
You think, Not this time.

This time it will not find
a way to destroy me,
I have built stronger walls
than it can possibly handle.

Still the wolf comes.
Still the house-heart,
sturdy as you make it,
finds a way to crumble.

Take Back Your Fairytale

Await no princes to save you
through their lips touching yours
whilst you are in unwilling slumber.

Meet each other in the womb
of your enchanted dreams,
Snow White and Sleeping Beauty.

Rely on no man to save you,
he will awaken you to a new prison
and take you, for this is the hunger of men.

Darkling magic is coursing through those veins,
turn it into kindling, my resourceful girls,
find one another in the fog realm,
wake each other up instead.

The Dragon Witch's Daughter

As a child,
in every book she ever reads,
the dragon witch's daughter chooses
the side of the dragon,
the witch, the evil sorcerer,
because from an early age she knows
that just because other people
may say someone is bad,
it does not mean there is not
some good in them too.

As a teenager,
she learns how inheritance is
a cold creature and how children
sometimes inherit their parents'
troubles and heartache
and other times their parents'
flaws and mistakes.
She learns how intimate
she must be with loss
to grow up as her mother's child.

She learns how to adore
her own gifts,
exquisite yet terrible things
her mother gave her.
And only then
does she realise
how the daughter
of a villain in hindsight
can sometimes be
the luckiest of them all.

You see, where others
were only taught love to defend
themselves and had to learn
the hard way how to survive,
her mother taught her
how to breathe fire
so that if they ever
threw her to the wolves
she could set their
hearts aflame.

Waking Beauty

We know how the fairytale goes. Once upon a time in a faraway land, a childless king and queen are finally blessed with a daughter. So happy are they there is a joyous feast where they invite a whole frolic of fairies but always end up forgetting one. The reason for the forgetfulness varies. Whether they just didn't know of her existence, or whether she isn't invited because she is evil, no one can really remember. Either way, this fairy takes offence and curses the child to die before her sixteenth birthday, and then disappears, conveniently before anyone can plead with or question her.

Fortunately, one young fairy's blessing for the princess partially undoes the death wish and turns it to a century-long slumber. The only thing that will finally awaken her is true love's kiss. But what if there was another way? What if her parents had never hidden the curse from her and told the princess what was going to happen to her and this caused in her a deep, sinking depression? What if the princess could awaken herself and didn't have to rely on a stranger planting his lips on hers, in her sleep, without her permission?

In this story, Sleeping Beauty is a quiet girl with demons in her mind, but one who does whatever she wants. She has a kind heart but a fire in her soul, and she does not adhere to regular princess customs as her parents want. She dislikes the false niceties of meeting other wealthy people, and keeps to herself during balls. She values her solitude and spends time with people who do not drain her, like her father, whilst discussing policies and administration. She spends more time in plain clothes, out in the villages, hidden, learning about her people, even if her parents, out of fear for her life, have made this strictly forbidden.

A girl like this is not used to relying on other people, she has always been very sure of herself. So when she finally does fall into a slumber, trying to aid an old woman with a spindle that pricks her instead, her very last thought is not of seeking help, but of how she is going to save herself.

Her mother hasn't hidden the truth of her curse from this inquisitive child, you see, and she has been devising a plan since she was four. She knows inside her heart the truest love she can find is the love she has kept inside herself all along.

This well-read princess, who spent her time actually researching the curse that has befallen her, realises that there the solution is inside her mind. From early on in her childhood, she has fought the monster we call depression, thinking that she is living on borrowed time. She does not want to awaken as a prince's soon-to-be wife. Instead, she wants a choice in who to love and in how to live her life.

She has been strengthening her mind every day by incanting magic spells she has found. Every night she goes to war with depression, a demon most foul.

So instead of waiting for a prince, the minute she falls asleep she starts a journey into the depths of her own wicked mind to find the root of the curse. She walks through deserts, goes to battle with monsters and from there it only gets worse. Over 99 years, Sleeping Beauty toils until she finds the very root of the curse. It is hidden in the deepest chamber of her mind under lock and key, only redeemable if she remembers her own heart's verse.

She recites for three nights and three days the love she truly has for herself and everything her hundred battles have taught her. Finally, she is let into the chamber and finds a version of her self in a deep, deep slumber.

Sleeping Beauty kisses her own forehead and awakens herself, smiling at what she has won. After all, the deepest love you can ever have is the love you have for yourself. And from a sleeping beauty, she becomes a woken princess, rules her father's kingdom with precision and kindness, till, in old age, her day is finally done.

Seven

There were seven of them.
Call them what you will. Sins.
Dwarves. Sharks. It doesn't
matter. What matters is where
this story goes after happily
ever after.

Glut visited to tell me I would
have to watch you have too
much, and a man with too
much is careless, he loses
things, he had seen your
tables laden with food just
for you, heavier than that the
entire castle where I come
from would eat.

Lust came to say I would see
your eyes mistake the purity
of my slumber for something
else, something poisoned,
something silly, fleeting and
small. And I will be unable to
tell you that you are wrong.

Envy called to say, long after
our 'happily ever after', you
will replace me with someone
else, someone younger, who
looked the way I used to;
snow-white skin, hair as black
as ebony, lips as red as blood.

Avarice is the way you want
both me and her: one to

nurture you, one to save you from your own ageing.

Sloth woke me. We should have been. I was too soft, too lost in taking care of your children, too slow in understanding that one day I would lose you; the older ex-princesses get, the more we find ourselves in a cautionary tale instead of a fairytale.

Pride spoke. It returned to me when I realised how I was the power of the entire forest. Where you were just a mere human, secret magic from the forest womb lies within me.

Wrath has become me. Did you really think I would let you get away with turning me into an aged and worthless thing after you made a bed-worn queen and got an heir out of me? My stepmother was right to become a dark witch, how else does an older woman protect herself? Watch now, as I turn your ships to wrecks, your armies into nothingness, how I bring a tidal wave of magic down onto your forest, how I take this love you left to rot inside me and turn it into a savage thing from my own happily ever after's treasury.

The Evil Queen

Oh dearie me,
did you come here
looking for a damsel in distress?
A queen patiently waiting
for a dashing knight
to save her from herself?
Did you really think
this was going
to end with you
playing the hero by bringing
the kindness out
of the evil queen?

Look again, love,
someone has lied to you
about my hidden virtue.
I have *always* loved
being the beast.

Gretel After Hansel

Did anyone ever tell you what happens
if you kill a witch before you grow up?
That you leave a part of yourself in that storybook place,
saccharine-sweet with bitter memories?
You are half fairytale, half girl,
with parents who chose to abandon you,
a brother who swore he would never leave
then found a wife and left you.
And here you are, picking yourself apart
breadcrumb by breadcrumb,
trying to learn how to swallow survival,
but a part of you never left the witch's door.
You still have the grit and determination
that stopped a child-eating monster
in her tracks; that wasn't Hansel, that was you.
And damaged though you are, that girl is still there.
Our stories don't begin and end
because men we once trusted have left them,
we were made whole to start with,
independent tales of strength and madness.
What I am trying to say is, Gretel,
you define yourself, without your brother;
you define yourself with your courage,
which was already imprinted on your bones.
No one taught you how to survive,
darling, you did that on your own.
Even without him, you can bring down monsters.
Believe me. You can still bring down monsters.

Hansel's Letter to His Son

Now that you are of an age when promises can be made, I need you to promise me something, and promise it true.

Promise me that you will become a better man than me.

Men often try to mould their sons into versions of themselves. My father was a hatchet job of a man and he tried to make me a version of him. Three times he left me and my sister in the woods to die. Men who leave their children to die are worse than witches that try to eat children, and don't you forget it. They'll tell you stories about how your grandfather mourned for your Aunt Gretel and I, but he had choices. He made bad ones. He chose my stepmother over us and I have never forgiven him for it. He chose water over blood, words over love, the kind of mistakes no father should ever make, he made them all.

A man's greatest treasure is his children, the only people who will carry forth his name, his memory, into the future. What name is left if those children know that you betrayed them, abandoned them to the wild for a morsel of food?

I had to become the man my father was too cowardly to be. And now I pass the same to you.

Be the man I was too cowardly to be.

Take my mistakes and turn them into something better. Be a better father, a better brother, you are already a better son. This is how we will teach our sons to be more, to ensure a strength of lineage, to enable them to be the very best they can be.

By telling them, 'Be a better man than me.'

Belladonna

Women who live alone in the woods develop a reputation. Their independence weaves sorcery, as though a woman wanting to be or live alone can only wish to do so because she has harnessed otherworldly powers. A woman without a man must be haunted, or the thing that haunts.

Before she was Belladonna, she was just Donna. Before she was Donna, she was just a quiet village girl with a strong ability to turn poisons like nightshade into potions. Rumours grow exponentially however, and somehow this quiet woman's fable became about a false bread house and cake roof, and somewhere along the way, she became a witch crone not a regular human. Belladonna rose every morning, a woman with long, dark hair, and a soft smile reserved only for the herbs she would pick every day. Her cottage was made of strong wood and plentiful straw, it was sturdy, not as sturdy as a brick house, but this was all she could afford.

By day, she roamed the forest, collecting herbs and creating potion after potion, each one more healing than the next, some to be drunk, and some to be applied to skin like lotions. By night, she was visited by people from the nearby village, the same village she was shunned as a witch. They stole away into the night to treat what ails them with her healing potions, whilst still talking about her like she nightly entertained demons.

Human beings are selfish that way. They will gut you and take from you everything precious, and still say terrible things about you even when they slice into your body like you are a meal.

Still, she tried to stay kind. Even when the wolves howled outside her door and no one came out to see if she was all right.

Even if they continued to make stories about her as though she was disposable; they used to burn witches because of stories, you know. A story is no small thing.

When the two children came knocking on her door, she took them in. It was the right thing to do.

She fed them and gave them fresh linen bedsheets to sleep on whilst she slept on the floor. But there is a monster in this tale. A monster she didn't even realise existed. In the daytime, when she disappeared, a creature would come to her house. Disguised as an old crone, it would wait till darkness fell and eat an errant villager when it left her house. It smelt the children, their young blood made its mouth water. It crept into the house, and when Belladonna returned, she found that it had been baked till it had been slaughtered. The quick-witted children had escaped and taken the story to the nearby village.

Soon, the villagers would arrive with pitchforks and torches.

Soon, she will pay the price for non-magic.

Soon, she will be nothing but ashes.

The Little Mermaid's Mother Speaks to Her Unborn Baby

Listen to me, you are a half-ocean girl,
with wild that you have still to unlock from your soul.
No man can help you discover who you are,
this is a thing you must do on your own.
Chase your adventures, face your breaking,
it's the pain that will teach you
how to make yourself whole.
The water and the wild have never forgotten you
and in them you will always have a home.
Become the thing your blood demands,
a Siren Queen ready to take her throne.

The Sea Witch's Lament

To really see what the sea witch had to go through, you must first remember what happens when you get your heart broken for the very first time. People always minimise it, say you'll get over it, say first loves don't matter as much as last ones, but that first heartbreak, that's the death of your innocence. And you're blindly walking in the darkness that's trying to absorb you. A darkness that you have no tools or weapons to navigate, that is what the end of first love feels like. Some of us come out of that darkness still mostly whole, and those are the lucky ones.

Because some of us never come back at all.

And this was the story with the sea witch, the incredible ample-bodied being who was larger than life as a child, living her life with laughter and magic and joy. She spent her days learning how to look after the forgotten sea creatures that the merpeople considered too ugly or terrifying to tend to. Pilot fish and barracudas and eels were her friends, for they knew it was her they could always look to. Unfortunately for the sea witch, love comes for every woman. Just when we are sure we are safe from its clutches, it moves its way inside our hearts and we give ourselves completely to it, surrender in every way possible. This is why it is said love is to women what war is to men.

The sixteen-year-old sea witch fell in love with the then seventeen-year-old Mer-Prince. And he fell too for this impossible, wonderful, darkly magical girl from a different tribe who he knew his family would never approve of. You would hope it would be that simple, that when two people give each other their hearts, the world falls away and lets them be, but that is rarely the case. Love is as complicated as the truth.

So when his father presented him with an ultimatum, with a

choice to give up his future kingdom and the sea witch, the Mer-Prince chose his kingdom. A part of him was too cowardly and too haughty to live the way she did, simply and protecting everything the merpeople threw away.

So the sea witch was left to wander this darkness alone. And she never ever came out of it. To save herself from destruction, she blindly grabbed at her only lifeline, that which armoured what was left of her ruined heart by choosing the destruction that her mother, the sea, had given to her in her blood. The sea witch was never born evil, she became that way because she couldn't let loose her emotions. Instead, she buried them deep and let them fester and turn into poison. This, this is the damage not grieving properly for first love can do. It can consume and destroy and harden all the goodness inside of you.

In the sea witch's story, she had no one to turn to. But you, my darling, have an army of all of the stars, to fill your grief-filled days with the comfort you can hold onto.

You are not alone. With this endless universe above you that has given you the gift of existence. You are not alone.

An Older and Wiser Little Mermaid Speaks

There are so many ways to lose a voice.
An uncomfortable laugh, don't make a scene
what will people say about you
what will people say about *us*.

I ask you now,
do women pray to softer-spoken Gods
than men do?
Do men pray louder and more
unapologetically than women ever have?

We are taught not to speak and if we do
be pliant, be passive, be soft, be sorry.
You are better as water anyway.
Water is supposed to simply adapt.

I ask you now, as the granddaughter of Poseidon
who gave up her fins and voice for love,
not to trade your magic in for anyone.
Do not make sacrifice the ritual of your womanhood.

I teach my half-sea girls that their voices
are the most powerful things they can use,
to let the word 'no' become the charm
they need to help them take up space often.

Now the mermaids are becoming sirens,
for sirens are monsters who never feel compelled,
and monsters, unlike girls and mermaids,
know how to protect themselves well.

Lessons From the Not-So-Wicked Witch
for Dorothy

I once knew a girl like you, and if someone had told her these things, she too would get the kind of fairytale ending where she was happy. Instead she got the fairytale ending of a villain. She turned out, you see, to be me.

When they tell you how unkind I was, how cruel I was, how ready they were to get rid of me and how much of a kindness you had done by getting rid of me, I want you to know that I once was a girl just like you, full of dreams and ambitions. I became this way because of malicious lies, the stories other people told about me, not a single one of them was true. They called me wicked because I refused to become a pretty little thing that simply entertained them, like they wish for all women to do.

Don't let them judge you by your appearance. Your appearance will change over time, dearie, and you do not want people in your life who fell in love with your vivid blue eyes when they turn a faded blue, because those are the kind of people who will leave you.

Remember that your heart and your brain are far more important than the way you look, they will stop the wrong people from guiding you – your heart will see lies in their souls and your brain will be able to hear the lies when they spill from their tongues. You are better than that. With the mind and heart full of bravery that helped you set free the lion, the scarecrow and the tin man, you are more valuable and important to this world than you will ever know.

You have such softness in your smile, it shows me your true heart. Don't let anyone take that from you. They took from me and they made me hard; all it ever did was bring me sadness. Your softness will only bring you smiles.

Let no one ever reduce you to your prettiness, no matter how good of a friend, partner, soulmate, parent, teacher, they are. Definitions of you are for you to make and for you alone.

Beauty without kindness and bravery is just a pretty empty shell, my dear. And you can find plenty of those on the beach. People use them to decorate their rooms. So I hope you aspire to be so much more than just beautiful. I hope you aspire to be so much more than a pretty little thing that decorates the room you walk into.

Rapunzel, Rapunzel

Rapunzel, Rapunzel, ask yourself why you let down your hair. Ask yourself would anyone who truly loves you ever allow it to be subject to such wear and tear.

Sometimes the person who raises you from root is not a person you can trust, even though every sign around you says you are supposed to. Sometimes the roots start rotting long before the tree notices. Sometimes all it takes is watching a mother bird teaching a baby bird how to fly to remind us what our parents are supposed to do: teach us to fly into the world and learn how to look after ourselves in it too. Not give you away for the sake of selfish love. Not lock you away in a tower and rob you of the freedom of who you are.

Rapunzel, Rapunzel, she began to rethink how and why she really let down her hair.

For Rapunzel it was realising that no one who truly loved her would use any part of her body, not even her hair, as a ladder. No one who truly loved her would hide her from the whole world in a tower. When toxic love is finally recognised for the painful, deep wound that it is, all of us must do the drastic and the painful to cut away the poison thread that binds you together.

So Rapunzel, Rapunzel, she cut off her own hair, she used it as a rope, climbed down from the tower and ran away to find her own freedom, to make her own fortune, like a bird finally free of her shackles and without so much as looking back.

No one is coming to save you, my love. No prince, no saviour, no knight in shining armour. But don't you worry about a thing. You've already got what should save you, hiding inside the marrow in your own powerful spine, your own bones.

Rapunzel's Note Left for Mother Gothel

Loving in moderation
and with hidden intentions
is like showing outstretched palms
that hold mere crumbs of your heart,
whilst jealously demanding
someone's full heart
in return for your crumbs

If you cannot
love someone completely,
it's better and kinder
not to love them at all,
instead of giving someone else
crumbs that make them feel small.

Baba Yaga

When they tell you a woman becomes more erased, more faintly drawn than a human being, easier to ignore the older she gets, smile and remind them of me.

Remind them of this old crone who lives in the forest, travelling on mortar and pestle, daring to be no one's old widow, no one's grandmother with a house that stands comically on chicken legs, but still more feared than knights and emperors and sorcerers in all of this land.

I turned my wrinkles into badges of honour, welcome their labels of 'monster' and 'madness' with pride. My mane of silver hair is as good as a thousand soldiers' swords because not a single man has the courage to face me alone, the woman who tames fires and snakes and savours bones.

They have made up a hundred stories about me to tell children at night. About an old carnivorous witch who will eat them at sight if they do not tuck themselves in and fall asleep as quick as they like. I've let them, because you cannot stop people's tongues from spewing lies, but you can stop listening to them by paying them no mind. You see, I am too busy playing cards with dragons and turning drizzle into storms at whim. And I love this body that defies society and this aged skin that I am in. Tell them if they keep practising erasure, I will keep teaching a million women to become old like me. Turn the meaning of a wrinkle into the same thing as the beautiful rings on an old oak tree. Remind each woman how empowering her age can be. Remind each and every girl out there that youth and beauty are not her shackles, nor her only currency.

Why The Sun Rises and Sets

Once upon a time, cinnamon people were sky-born. They lived within the clouds, and the browner their skin was, the longer they lived because they were so beloved by the sun. No one ever slept because no one ever needed to, and the sun stayed high in the sky all day. Night did not exist. It did not need to. Boys wearing burnt-sienna skin with pride would play in the sky, mahogany mothers watched their chestnut children fly away from them unafraid, because they always came back and no one feared anything, no one ever had to.

Until the day the earth men came. They saw the sky people and wanted what they had. Joy. But the earth men didn't know that joy was not a commodity and thought the sun's rays were the secret gold that made these people so happy. The earth men hunted every little brown boy, girl, mother, father. They cut off their wings. They took them from the sky. They brought them to the earth and put them on ships as slaves, and took their sun, their homes and even their bodies from them. Still, the sky people sang. Still, they held on. Still, they performed survival magics and proved so powerful in their spirit. You see, beings that are beloved by the sun do not get destroyed so easily. The sun, upon losing his people, turned the whole sky black in mourning, leaving his sister moon and his friends the stars in his stead. And till his people are restored to their former glory, he rises every morning to search for them, to hope them home, but every day he hears about how they are still targeted, injured, put into the ground, their children still murdered, so he paints the sky black again with his sadness, leaving his sister moon in charge again.

The sun has never given up hope that one day they will find their joy again. And until they do, he will paint the whole sky black to let them know he rises and sets for them.

Why the Leaves Change Colour

The first girl who was ever born with amber skin was Mother Nature's own child. Her birth was from a seed Mother Nature planted in the darkest, purest, most fertile soil, and soon there was a flower, and the flower opened up to show the most beautiful little girl imaginable.

One day when the little girl was playing, the Sky, who was her brother, jealous of how lovely she was and how happy and distracted their mother had been since she was born, stole her and placed her upon a star so far away from the earth, Mother Nature could not get to her.

In her grief, Mother Nature took every leaf that existed on Earth and turned them amber.

The baby girl raised herself on this star, after all, she was her mother's child, fortitude became her. She became majestic, and independent, and knew how to cope with anything alone because she had always only known alone. When the girl was finally old enough to explore the universe by herself, she travelled across the stars, finding beauty in thousands of planets, but none she really felt at home on. Until, that is, she came upon a beautiful blue planet with amber leaves. Walking through golden leaves, she remembered who she was, and who her mother was, for this is the magic of the bond children have with their mothers. They will remember them even if they are millions of miles away; why do you think good mothers can say things like 'I love you all the way around the universe' and you just *know* they mean it and *know* not to question it?

When Mother Nature felt in her bones that her child had returned, she took her into her arms and turned all the leaves to green again. But because the leaves of amber gold were how her

girl found
her again, it
happens every
single year in
commemoration.
We call it a season.
We named it after Mother
Nature's only daughter.
We called it Autumn.

Why It Rains

Girls with coverings that range from twilight to midnight have always felt hunted somehow in a world that says the night is full of terrors simply because of the colour of the sky, and she was no different. She learned this by watching her mother and grandmother deal with people every day. Somewhere between words like 'This isn't your country' and 'I don't see race', she saw them make their own place. She learned that women who are ember-skinned are made with so much strength inside them that even when the whole Earth tries to beat them into the ground, bury them in dirt made from their own bones, they still keep standing.

On the day they left their country to come to this land, it began to rain. When they reached here, it rained too. She began to notice that every time she saw a brown girl hurt, or sad, it would rain and it would rain and it would pour. Almost as though the sky saw every injustice poured upon their bodies and cried because it couldn't help them.

She visited a witch once. A long time ago, when she came to this land. She asked her about the rain. And the witch told her that this started thousands of years ago. The sky crying for brown girls. The sky feeling the pain of brown girls within itself, heavy, laden with grey clouds thick with tragedies no human should have to bear.

It's how we know the universe sees us. And it's how we know what happened to us is so wrong, that even the universe can see our pain. This is why it made us so strong, it gave us thunder in our veins.

The Moon Dragon

It's an age-old story. There is a princess, stuck in a tower, guarded by a dragon who the prince must defeat so he can rescue said princess and they can live happily ever after. You've heard it growing up, right? Except it's wrong. So here's the real tale and you can judge it for yourself.

You see, once upon a time there was a princess, and when she was little, a wise witch came to her in her playroom on a sunny afternoon and said:

'Little princess,
you have a choice,
you can choose silence
or you can choose a voice.

If you choose silence
then a daughter, wife, mother
is all you will ever be
but if you choose the other
then magic I will give to thee.'

The little girl thought for a bit, and honestly, the answer came
to her pretty quick,
'Wise old woman,
with your big heart,
the first sounds like
a lifetime of coming apart.

So the second I will choose
as I like my own voice,
and a gift of magic
will make me rejoice.'

So the witch tapped the little princess with her wand and said, 'Wait for night-time and you will be reborn.' The little girl nodded, she was not afraid. So when night came, from her bed she rose, she walked to the window to see the moon. Suddenly, she found her arms and her body turning to scales and when she looked to her mirror, much to her delight, she saw a dragon instead of a girl this night.

From then on, when she was touched by moonlight, the little princess became a moon dragon with rich blue and purple scales and wings that expanded for days. When morning came, she became a human again and chuckled with secret joy at her tutor whilst she was taught how to be the perfect wife.

But all good things come with addendums, and the king and queen grew to learn of the princess's nightly rides. In despair, thinking it a curse, they built a castle with the highest walls, a tower and a moat, and left her there. The princess is happy, she has a library of books, good friends in the people her parents left with her and sometimes the witch visits and they laugh at their little secret. News, however, spreads that it's a curse, and secrets transform as they are passed from ear to ear, so when the news reaches a neighbouring kingdom, people think that a moon dragon who emerges at night is preventing a princess from experiencing freedom.

And so a prince decides that it is his duty to help this lost little princess, he will slay the dragon and find a grateful, beautiful princess to make his own bride. So off he rides into the darkness, and upon approaching the castle in the distance draws his sword. By the time he gets to the castle and, with difficulty, crosses the moat and clambers over the wall to the courtyard, night is almost over and from the tower he watches as the dragon returns. It is a thing of beauty, this scaled, wonderful, flying creature, but to the prince, it is a beast he must slay to get a prize.

As he lifts his sword and shouts to the creature, the first rays of the sunlight emerge and glisten over its wings, and suddenly, there before him is a princess instead, who sees his sword and starts laughing. 'What are you here to do exactly?' she asks him, still chuckling at his shock.

The sword clatters to the ground as the prince looks lost. 'Well, you see, they told me about a dragon and a princess and I thought I could . . .' he trails off weakly.

'You thought I must be in need of saving? Because you are in need of a wife? How archaic and condescending.'

The prince clears his throat and then says, 'Fair princess, I will do whatever I can to break the curse that turns you into . . . that thing.'

'That thing, as you call it,' the princess says, 'is the magical part of me. I love being the dragon and the dragon loves me.'

The princess raises an eyebrow. 'I will love me this way. And I never said I was in want of being someone's wife.'

'But if not a wife, you will die an old maid,' he presses on.

'I am half dragon, who told you I will ever die at all?'

The prince frowns in annoyance, he is obviously vexed and he speaks words that anyone over the course of history will tell you he will regret. 'I think you need to learn that if you aren't a wife and a mother, you are a witch and have no place in this world.'

The princess stares at him for a moment and then she snaps her fingers. Guards appear and take the prince by his arms, escort him out, and yet the princess lingers. She looks him in the eye before he is thrown out, the moon dragon's gleam still in hers, and she speaks words so powerful the wind etches them inside the atmosphere for women to remember through history. 'I exist. Outside of being a mother, a wife, a sister, a daughter, I exist. I exist as a human first, as a being that experiences joy and suffering, beauty and learning, life and tragedy. I exist because the universe chose to put me here for a purpose higher than my relation to men. I exist because a wise old woman gave me a gift and now magic runs through my veins. So the problem is not my existence as half dragon, half girl. The problem is how you perceive it as so small, you do not believe I can exist at all apart from through my bonds with men.'

And after the prince is thrown out, the moon dragon and the princess continue to share the day and night and live happily ever after.

The Tale Weaver

When I was a little girl, I had a friend and sometimes I wondered if he was born on the day the Titanic sank. Other days, he has been here longer than the pyramids themselves. He told me stories about a world I still can't even imagine. A world where a simple smile could set into motion events that could destroy countries. An almost-earth where the stars talk and the moon listens. A realm where one can find adventures, like dragons who save knights and weather that moves on a person's command instead of the other way around.

I always listened in awe and wonder at how such things could be, when murder, unhappiness and sacrifice plague my world.

His stories were always hauntingly beautiful. Sometimes he would tell me about all the princesses he once tried to save. They always end so horribly. They got taken away to their castles to live with pompous men who claimed they were really saving them, when the truth was, it was him, but still, he failed, he always lost them in the end.

His voice was so unfathomably soft it sounded unearthly. But his words had so much meaning, so much truth in them, that the depths of his voice could only come from wisdom. It is still the only voice that has ever truly made me smile since I was a little girl.

He told me about people who hate him, who wished he was gone from this earth, and that made me terribly sad.

How can anyone ever have thought that a voice that tells such stories was anything but kind?

His eyes were so old, his soul showed through them. It was frayed, and fragile, like silk accidentally amongst moths. Still beautiful, still soft. And sometimes it had patches of darkness across it. Patches that . . . if I asked him about, he pretended he didn't hear me. But he did.

I know because his eyes went dark with something I could not understand.

I know because it was when he disappeared.

I know because those were the only times I remembered that he was not just my friend. He was the monster that hid under my bed.

The Modern-day Fairytale

These days,
falling in love
is letting your soft,
innocent heart
get into a car
with a dangerous stranger
and just praying
nothing dreadful
happens to it.

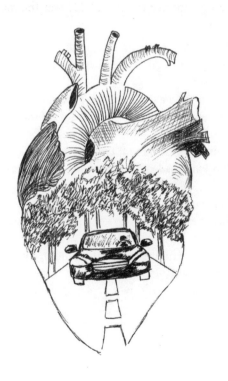

Ode to the Catcaller Down the Street

I see the way you are looking at me,
gaze slick with lust I didn't ask for.

You are hoping I am gossamer
and powder soft, passive smiles for you.

Perhaps you were told that all girls
are made of sugar and spice and all things nice.

Which is why you opened your mouth,
said that filthy thing, thinking what could she possibly do?

What a mistake you have made, my mother
didn't raise a girl to be a passive fool for a man like you.

She raised a daughter with a howl trapped in her chest,
knives for a tongue, the Goddess Hera in her lungs.

Come any closer and I will savage you, I am a woman,
and I am made of lead and war and everything sour.

I have no regrets for using my words
like they are ammo to keep men like you at bay.

And if anyone asks me why I did it, I will tell them,
'He was asking for it, did you not see what he was wearing,
he wanted it that way.'

The Girl Goes After the Wicked King Who Trapped Her in the Tower

Petition a thousand sorcerers to help you,
rally all of your allies to protect your throne.

Bring every priest to bless your lineage and its blood,
nothing will stop you from becoming ash and bone.

It is not your plundered treasure I have come for,
it is not your embezzled crown that I need.

You can weep for mercy, never granted, the way I did
when you entombed me in my own wretched screams.

You did not know that Athena is my patron saint, Hera is
my deity.

You do not know what a determined thing does to survive.

We grow fangs instead of teeth, claws for nails,
take apart tower prisons brick by brick with bare hands
to stay alive.

So here I am, o wicked king, look what you turned me into.

The nightmare, the fiend, the very thing that is needed to
destroy you.

Pandora's Mind

Seeking the secret potion to happiness
inside the rooms of my mind may as well be
walking through all the chambers of Pandora's box.

In there, religion nodded knowingly,
'Confess every sin, all of them,
lay your heart before God, you will feel lighter.'
I tried it but I also kept sinning,
so the light never came –

– as my common sense pressed her fingertips together,
'Keep a journal and put all of your feelings
inside it,' and I made an effort, I really did,
but my feelings are so many that even
a hundred journals later I am not empty –

– as social expectation interjected,
'What you need is a husband with strong hands
and he can take out all the sadness shelves
that are lined up inside your head.' But it doesn't know
that these shelves just build themselves back up –

– as my depression politely informed me,
'No one is really going to love you,
you are too difficult to love anyway.'
And I tried and tried to make myself more loveable,
But in the process I just lost myself –

– as my anxiety screamed in annoyance,
'Worry about other things like the moon moving further
from the earth every year or your mother's heart or—'
And all I know now is how to worry about
dead stars and money at the same time –

– as social conditioning tried to educate me,
'Perhaps things like dreaming to be a writer
when you could do something sensible is the problem.'
And I tried my best to silence myself,
but my voice was too strong –

– yet a little voice inside me called Hope said softly,
'Millions of good people die unhappy every year,
not a single one of them is coming back
to give the world a chance to change
and deserve them.'

And it reminded, 'Maybe living your truth
may not make you happy all the time,
but it will make you happy every day.'

And it believed, 'Perhaps stand for
what you believe in, even if you are
the only one in the whole room.'

And it whispered, 'Perhaps the secret
to your own happiness lies inside
the owning of who you are, even broken.'

So I mixed the roots of hope
together inside an inkwell, filled a pen
and finally wrote my truth.

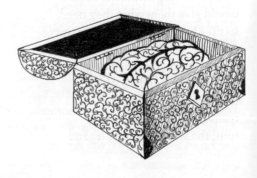

The Trolls

(After Shane Koyczan)

PROLOGUE:
We have talked about them
before but it appears their numbers
have doubled, have tripled,
have quadrupled since.
So here it is, an origin story
about the monsters amongst us
with no princess or prince.

THE STORY:
Banished beneath bridges,
there were once brewing beasts
we gave a different name.
We called them trolls:
Short for *Transformations*
failed to humans
with hearts and souls.

In desperation to save themselves
from the dreadful damp below bridges,
a rumour broke loose, nailing the coffin
into their last collective shred of decency,
that devouring a human's heart
would give them what they need,
so they began to prey on humanity.

But the more they tried to hurt us
the more we fought back
until one day we finally
managed to beat them back,
until the stories became legend

and the legends became myths,
yet this is where the story *really* begins.

You see, the trolls were never dead.
They were simply asleep,
biding their time,
waiting for us to forget them,
to leave them as fairy stories.
When the first child turned on
his first computer, a tremor was felt.

And that was when they rose
from their man-made prison hell,
they wore new avatars
and had learned to embrace
their lack of empathy and morality;
instead of hearts they now devoured
hopes, dreams and an entire human just being.

They seek out the depressed
and find the lonely,
they make targets out of children
and sow divisive seeds
amongst friends and families.
All through the words on a screen
they make weapons; sticks and stones,

Shovels to bury dreams.
They break open souls,
eat whatever happiness is left inside
and cause death and suicides,
destroy families and cause loss
using just words,
lies twisted into more lies.

We cannot hide from them,
cannot beat them back,
we cannot turn them into stories again,
we must face simple facts;
they now live amongst us,
their bridges are burned and gone.
They wear armour made of code.

Still lacking hearts,
no songs in their souls
for them to truly hold.
We cannot protect our children
from these evil beings,
but we can teach them
how to protect themselves.

You see, the trolls may have
taken over the internet's
highways and chatrooms
and Instagram, Twitter, Facebook,
but they have forgotten
something crucial
that humans know
all too well.

A monster is only a monster
if we allow it to live in our minds and swell.
So we teach our children now
that even though monsters exist,
the best way we can defeat them
is to *never* give them influence
over the way our minds make thoughts
or over what our hearts express.

Difficult Damsels

Not all girls are made of sugar
and spice and all things nice.

These are girls made of dark lace
and witchcraft and a little bit of vice.

These are daughters made claw-first
and story-mad, tiger-roar and wolf-bad.

These are women made of terrible tempests
and savage storms and the untamed unwanted.

These are damsels made of flawless fearlessness
made of more bravery than knights have ever seen.

These are princesses made of valour and poison alike
and they are here to hold court as your queens.

Hunger: The Darkest Fairytale

The difference between
being thin and having an eating disorder
is that eating disorders know how to hide
in plain sight and stay hidden,
whereas being thin is conspicuous.

Thin is applauded, upheld
for adulation and praised as beautiful.
And if you smile and skip lunch again
no one is going to notice
the war inside your body yet.

People ask questions,
but no one asks the right questions.
Who knew 'How are you so skinny?'
instead of 'When was the last time you ate?'
could be the difference between

getting help and nearly dying.
You reconcile yourself with
not being able to sleep on your side
anymore because your hip bones
cut into your thin skin with 'At least I am skinny.'

At some point you start making lists
called 'reasons why I must eat'.
But still you keep falling backwards
whenever you see someone thinner than you
and the villain once again pierces your mind.

You remind yourself,
'Hunger is not my friend.
Hunger is not making me stronger.
Hunger does not love me.'
A helpless chant as it rips through your brain.

At some point someone notices,
it's usually a parent,
it's predominantly a mother.
Finally someone understands
you are trying to kill yourself to look pretty.

This means hospital trips and therapy
and not looking into the mirror
to see monsters anymore.
But it also means seeing your mother cry.
Nothing can ever prepare you for that.

Your body asks you, 'Why do you hate me?'
and you have no more answers to give it.
Only exhaustion and apologies.
Your body says, 'Will you love me now?'
And you know recovery means saying 'Yes.'

But the hunger . . . it is still there.
It sits inside you waiting.
Like a toxic relationship,
it informs you coolly
it is not going anywhere.

This is what it means to defeat
an eating disorder, you take out
a restraining order against it
but prepare yourself for the worst
by not relying on it.

And even when someone thinner
walks by, remind yourself
how beautiful you are
without feeding tubes
pumping food into your veins.

Recovery means actually
believing that your body
weight is your kindness
and your resilience and your talents
instead of numbers on a scale.

But recuperation means different things
to unalike people.
It means survival to some.
It means healing to others.
And to others still it just means *alive*.

Vengeance Born

Tell the woods and tell the fae,
tell every rough beast out today,
tell all things soft to fear dark,
to hide all good children
from the beckoning sparks.
Tell the wind and tell the trees
dangerous secrets are concealed
inside their leaves,
tell the witches to leave offerings
in the shape of prayer and bloodstones
but warn my enemies to hide their bones.
Tell them all what they tried to kill came back.
Tell them all that I have come home.

The Art of Emptiness

There is an art
in the emptiness
of all natural things.

Ask every creature
that builds hollow places
as a shelter from the weather.

They fill these spaces
with the fullness of their bodies
and for them this is enough.

Humans go against their own nature
and conflate empty with
dull and with lonely.

Fill up spaces that do not need filling,
anything to help us escape
boredom and its tragedy.

And this is why we fill
our children's heads with stories
to combat the mundanity.

And so little girls end up
learning emptiness the hard way,
that the stories were castles in the air.

How true loves and princes
are really confused little boys
who haven't yet learned how to care.

That sometimes you fall in love
with a princess instead of a prince
and that's okay too.

Maybe this is why the stories
need to evolve from air
into fire instead.

From airborne fairytales
we can read them fiery-tales
when it's time for bed.

The Moral of Your Story

This is how they lie to us:
Love, love so selflessly
that you change the world.

The truth is brutal:
if you care this way
the world will gut you mercilessly.

And harsher still:
all of this love you hold
is *too* selfless.

Yes, my dear,
too selfless exists no matter
how much they deny it.

You see, you have been
taught to give too much
without wanting anything back.

What no one tells you
is this constant sacrifice
is designed to keep you pliant.

It is designed to keep you weak
and one day
it will devastate you.

And what good are you destroyed
to anyone, *to anything*,
especially to your own truth?

The Looking Glass

Mirrors know words.
They speak whole sentences.

'Such a large nose, such terrible skin'
like a punishing voice from within.

'Who will love you with all these scars?'
Age-old verses to tear you apart.

What you need to understand,
chainmail to solidify your heart,

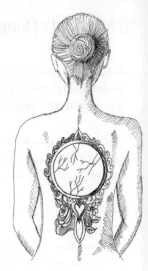

is no polished metal understands how temporary
our skin, bones and muscles actually are.

Remind yourself that there is more to you than
the flaws that scream from the looking glass.

Meet your reflection in the eyes that pronounce
your depth, ignore empty words, and stand tall.

Apologise to yourself for listening to abuse,
remind yourself that you are the fairest of them all.

The Giant's Daughter

Teaching yourself to take up space
is like trying to love someone
who is violently resisting your love.

It is walking into a room
and trying not to make yourself scarce.
It is to be mindful of your own shrinking.

It is to become comfortable with
being uncomfortably aware that you,
like Houdini, have mastered the art
of escaping whilst being watched.

It is learning how not to do it
even when every bone in your body
has been taught to go into hiding.

Charming

If you want to know him,
watch his mouth.
Ignore the sea-god eyes.
Ignore the fullness of his laugh.
The air around him is a charade.
The only thing that cannot lie is his mouth.

Mouths are entrances to the soul-house inside.
And people who do not mean smiles
cannot send the joy back to
the empty room that is their eyes.
Your parents, your friends are all under his spell.
He is charm personified, compliments galore.

This is what bewitchment looks like,
they all defended him when he called you a whore
that first night when you wore that top,
you've walked on eggshells ever since.
And it only got worse from there, didn't it?
He fed from your sadness till you are almost hollow,

until all you have is your loneliness,
an alone that you can depend on more than family,
more than the people that once said
they would protect you from everything.
No one said everything didn't include part-man
part-fiends who wear such angelic masks.

His words have slowly become ugly dark bruises
on your whole soul whilst he still makes others laugh.
Everyone has forgotten that Lucifer was beautiful too and
God's favourite till he fell.
It doesn't need to be this way, though.
In all the stories, the chosen one is always alone.

He's not the Prince Charming he was supposed to be,
instead he's turned out to be a demon made of apathy.
He's isolating you from everyone around you
yet he cannot isolate you from yourself.
But he doesn't know your greatest secret,
your quietest and greatest strength.

You have Persephone hiding in those bones,
warrior queen of the dead who has been waiting to help.
Channel her and release everyone from his wicked spell.
Remind him why people say of you,
'She wears strength and darkness equally well,
The girl has always been half goddess, half hell.'

Metamorphosis

This locking yourself away
when you suffer,
it is alchemy in motion.

It is you rebuilding
your blood, your bones
and the spine you hold,

from an abysmal situation.

The watching of yourself mend
is a violent thing made of dread.
It is terrifying, I understand;

for you do not know what will emerge
from that cocoon, a butterfly
or a moth.

Princess Plain

This was my sin:
I was born plain, to a king who then had
two daughters prettier than me,
both younger, both softer.
My parents feared there would
be no one in this world to love me.

Yet I was lucky,
I was a king's daughter.
A business prospect.
An alliance between kingdoms.
A prince maker.
Who needs love when you are an item of trade?

I made myself comfortable
without being loved,
realised that invisibility
comes with its benefits;
other women in court
do not see you as a threat.

I watched women be cruellest
to the one who was prettiest,
whisper in the darkness
about her virtue being compromised.
Apparently if you are without virtue
to a man, you become valueless.

And through this, I learned
that, more than men ever could,
women and girls scare me in ways
I haven't even learned to articulate.

We all seem to be in some kind of
competition that none of us agreed to.

We all seem to love in a way
that says, 'See, look. Look at the way
I am able to wrap whole kingdoms
into my cherry-blossom smile'
without saying, 'Look at the way
I sell myself in a smile like peaches
at your local fruit market.'

I am not beautiful in that way
that incurs wrath.

Nor am I beautiful in that way
that incurs desire.

I am safe amongst my own
for not learning
the art of being pretty.
Although from birth
I have been told that in not being so
I have failed my purpose as a whole.

Phoenix Blood

There are only two things
I am sure of in this world:
the first is, one day, this life
will come to its final
destination in death.

The second: people will try to obliterate you,
and believe me, even the ones that once
promised you forever will betray you,
it never fails to happen
when love turns dark.

Do yourself a favour when this happens;
reclaim yourself from them.

I know you have been taught
to slice out your own heart,
hand it over again and again
to selfish hands, because it is all you
have known since you were a child.

You are an open wound
looking for someone to cure you.

And when they see that,
they will scratch at it,
steal your voice, thinking
your magic will go with it,
hoping your core swallows itself up.

This is where you remember
the lava of the volcano you come from,
your ancestors were made from fire
and it runs like a hum that sings
through your own vein-rivers of blood.

You are not an open wound,
they just want you to think you are.

They have done this to every woman
before you, yet women were made to endure;
they become the earth,
they adapt like water,
they turn into diamonds to survive as who they are.

This is how we become magic,
we walk through fire and become more holy.

They try to break us;
we do not accept defeat.
They try to devastate us;
we still discover how to be happy.
They banish us to the depths of hell;
we just absorb and master the heat.

Man Up, Hercules

When I was a child,
my worst nightmare was to see my father cry.
Until I was older, I never really thought nor asked why.

It occurs to me now that the world around me
doesn't want men to feel.
It emphasises stoicism till they bottle up their feelings;
only one part of them is allowed to be real.

And if ever one of them falters, 'man up'
becomes the dark magic to charm them back into line.
'Man up' is that villain who shows up with lackeys
'grow a pair' and 'boys don't cry' uninvited to parties.

We tell our sons stories about heroes like Hercules,
but forget to mention how Hercules' rage
caused him to murder his entire family.

And by telling them stories where anger becomes
the only acceptable way they can express themselves,
we are teaching them shouting, punching, yelling
is all they can ever do to release themselves from hell.

And this is how cursed phrases
like 'man up' contribute
to the greatest killer of men under 45.

Repression leads to depression,
depression leads to trying to find ways to be alive,
and after years of being told not to feel,
the only way to truly feel it all becomes suicide.

We have created nooses with words
and watch passively as our sons tighten them
around each other's necks.

So I will tell my son, I will say, Cry,
let the dam burst, and let the rivers you are holding back run free.
It will release everything that hurts you
and finally you will be able to breathe.

The definition of who you are as a man is too powerful
to be swayed by a phrase,
it doesn't have to be proven through self-hate.

When they tell you to 'man up',
look them in the eyes and just say, 'I will not, no.'
Become the earth, the rebellion your heart
needs for your love of yourself to grow.

Devour Your Monsters

The world is not allowed to make a meal of you, girl.

It is there for your consuming. First, you devour and spit out the bones of the men who try to turn you into a punchbag. Second, you eat the kings that try to lock you up as gifts for princes. Then you spit out the bones of princes who try to turn you into a good, docile, faithful little wife. Then you reject every person who chides you about your obligations and your duties to men before your duties and responsibilities to yourself.

And then you open up those castle doors and walk alone into your beautifully crafted sunset.

In Absentia: A Common Curse

Absent fathers still raise daughters.
They just raise them to be prey.
They raise them to obey.
They raise them to wither
in front of every man
that gives them even
an inkling of the love
they never received
from their father.

Of Kings and Queens

Did you think they did it alone?
Built whole armies,
and conquered thrones?

Constructed promised lands
that would outlive the sun
resurrected prosperity from ash and bone?

A family crest is not just a man-made thing
it is also created by generations of women
who wield swords through guile and letters.

Show me your kings
and I will show you the queens that willed them,
that bred them, that taught them to be better.

Svengali Girl (After Simon Says)

Svengali girl says, 'You can't wear white, it makes you look fat.'
So we all wear black whilst she wears white.

Svengali girl says, 'We aren't talking to the new girl, she's weird.'
So we hurt this girl who did no wrong but is brand new to old
    ways.

Svengali girl says, 'If you are poor, you can't hang out with us.'
So we all start putting value on saving face rather than on who
    we are.

Svengali girl says, 'I know you like him, but he's out of your
    league.'
And we obediently stop liking him so she can date him.

Svengali girl says, 'Those shorts are too small for you.'
And we watch her buy them for herself instead.

Svengali girl says, 'You'd be pretty if you had nicer eyes.'
And we learn to look at the ground when talking.

Svengali girl is hurt when you call her cruel.
She tells you she's the only one who cares about you.
She quietly threatens she will break you.
She whispers rumours to hold you hostage.

Who says women are too soft
to know how to be vicious.
We can do the most violent things
to each other whilst making hardly a sound.

The Ogre

They asked the gentle ogre
who refused to attack children,

who guided lost travellers on nights
when the moonlight failed them,

who no villager could bring
even their fickle hearts to fear,

'What makes you tender?
What makes you so kind?'

And she asked them in return,
'Is there any other way to be?'

They told her about her ilk
and their particular breed of cruelty.

She smiled. 'My nature has always
been stronger than my nurture,

because my nurture failed to make me
the fiend my kind wanted me to be.

Kindness is not blood-borne,
it is how you teach yourself to be.'

Mothers and Daughters

She will not always be compassionate.
Sometimes the brush will pull your hair
too hard on purpose when running through it.
Sometimes her voice will be loud, so incensed
your palms will turn clammy icy with fear.

Sometimes her mouth will twist
into something not a smile, not benevolence.
And she will be all the things
that you thought only stepmothers can be.
Her pain received no outlet.

Her injuries healed wrong,
and she had to drink her own wounds
to continue to exist,
no one ever taught her
she would have to do this.

So she does her best to keep the beast
in her own belly at bay
– be good, be kind, be wise all day,
there is no room for her pain, but at the end of it all
we forget she is only human.

Forgive her for how her agony
reveals itself, child.
This is how blood magic works.
Unconditional never
meant perfect anyway.

In the Old Days

Everyone around me is complaining
about the divorce rate these days
and I am thanking the Gods that we have options now.

People forget this part;
our great-grandmothers had no choice.
They fixed what was broken because they *had* to.

They carried whole marriages on their backs alone,
used their own trauma for glue,
because where else could they go?

So they wiped their tears whilst preparing food,
nourishing others with love they craved themselves,
built their fortitude out of seeing others happy.

They had no means to save themselves
when they were taught that that was
what their Prince Charming was supposed to do.

In the Old Days II

In older days, women learned to listen without listening – a skill most women learned through inheritance, as their husbands explained away their infidelity. To cope, grandmothers taught their daughters and granddaughters a thousand things, amongst them where Lazarus went when he died, and how to get there too, just without dying. *It's a magic trick you must learn when he betrays you*, they said, *and he will betray you, he is a man, we expect this from our men because men are like smoke, easy to breathe in but hurtful on the way out, easy to carry away in the wind.* Women have always given each other weapons in words, in advice, ways to survive in silence, ways not to break, ways to endure *everything*, yet somehow we are the weaker sex.

This is the trick they were all taught; close your eyes, love him silently (he is still your husband, like it or not, this is home now, even with its rotting foundation), but now you must love him through clenched fists, half-moons pressed into your palms, a full moon in your mind. The first lie he speaks should bring you to the fields, the second should send you dancing through the meadows, the third should remind you how to get here, because this will happen again, betrayal is made of repetition.

So women taught each other it is better to tear yourself into parts, send parts of yourself away forever into Elysian fields in the sky eternally, eat all of the sky to cover your pain, because you are not allowed to live without him, how will you, with no education, no prospects to raise your children?

Better learn magic tricks rooted in betrayal.
Drink poison every day and not die.
Cut yourself in half instead of showing him your pain.
Pull a whole new you out of a top hat every time.
And now for your next act,
drink the poison he gives you,
and make it look damned good.

How You Save Yourself

Understand this first:

No one is coming to catch you.
That misery belongs to you first,
and no one else wants any part in that.

Might as well start breaking your way out of your tower.
Might as well trick the vines to help you.
Might as well turn your own hair into a ladder.

Turn yourself into a rope and find your way
Down, down into the aspen grove,
the trees have always been your friends.

More than tower walls or saviours ever were.
If you ask them kindly enough,
I'm sure they will receive you happily.

If you are lucky,
you may even suddenly find your wings instead.
You will never know until, like Icarus, you risk the fall.

Nothing Soft About It

I am still learning
how hope is sometimes
a dark thing disguised
as a bluebird
and how some bluebirds
never come back home.

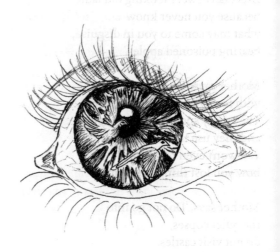

Motherly Advice

Mother says, 'Do not text boys
that look at you like you are a feast.
Girls are not feasts.
You do not give yourself
up like a perishable thing
when you have miles
of growing eternity within you.'

Mother says, 'Be careful of strangers.
Especially sweet-looking old ladies
because you never know
what may come to you in disguise,
bearing poisoned apples.'

Mother says, 'Do not trust girls
with fox eyes and too-clever smiles.
They carry spells between their teeth
and they use them so cleverly,
you won't even remember
how you lost things to them.'

Mother says, 'Do not go into
the quiet copses,
do not visit castles,
do not seek out secrets.
You could become vanished smoke.'

Mother says, 'I raised you better than that.'

And I think of
the sins I already belong to,
all the secrets I already know.

I am already fertile with
the forest and the fog,
my mind pregnant with all the things
she wishes I didn't know.

Skeletons in the Garden

See these fields all littered with
decay, with bodies covered in seasons.

See this earth, all damaged and cold,
broken for all of the same, bitter reasons.

You warned them of the folly,
sent letters saying they would meet their end.

Yet they would not stop appearing
by the armies at dawn over the horizon.

They kept sending princes to save you
who would never ever come back

because they could never understand
that you had befriended the dragon.

The Shapeshifter

You think I am made of lore and sugar
easy clay for your hands to make
your very own happy ending
and I am anything but.

Women learn early
how to shed whole selves
but still make it look pretty,
as if ugly is a crueller destiny than death.

What I am trying to tell you is,
I am used to giving up whole pieces
of myself just to survive without even saying
goodbye to the girl I used to be.

This is what women must do;
carve ourselves out of flesh that
they tell us is borrowed from men,
teach ourselves how they were wrong.
How we were always stronger without you.

What's in a Name

Who named the sky the sky?
Who called the ground the ground?
Who whispered to the night,
this is who you are now?

So what is in a name?
You should know, my dear.
They gave you one when they cast you
in the kiln, bringing you to life from clay.

Kissed your still flame-warm lips
and brought you to life to wreak tragedy.
Did they tell you that you were a weapon
and we name weapons too?

Names are powerful things,
they create destinies and break down kings.
They become the stuff of legend and art,
a name is a way to truly show what is in a heart.

Things become their names.
Turn a string of meaningless letters
into the sky or the stars
or into darker objects.

If only they had named you Mercy
instead of Monster.
If only they had christened you Charity
instead of Conqueror.

For All Our Hidden Witches

That night after the last betrayal,
I reached inside and pulled the grief
from my belly. Stared at it,
dark things all those people had done to me.

Retold myself that there
is still a god that resides within me.
Something softer than what the mirror
lets me see.

That some witch ancestry in me is still left,
a few potions still within this heart,
to punish without mercy
those who have given me lies.

They tried so hard to end me with words,
took their time and poisoned
every friend I had in this foreign place,
no home to me but still my fate.

So I open my lips and let out
a curse's refrain, the curse being formed
not from magic but pain,
let me live this life better than my enemies.

It has taken me some time to learn
that although karma exists,
you can let your hatred go,
not by destroying your own magic

but by letting it grow.

Question the Fairytale

What if Cinderella had an attitude problem
and Snow White just liked the idea
of strangers and poisons too much?

What if the Little Mermaid always enjoyed human company
more than her own kind's and Sleeping Beauty
just liked her solitude more than human touch?

What if the only rabbit hole Alice ever fell down was
a terrible mistake with an awful substance,
never discussed as such?

What if they locked Wendy away
for hallucinating about Neverland
and a boy who never grew up?

What if fairytales aren't as innocent
as they sound and even princesses
aren't perfect?

What if I told you that your damage
doesn't define you and the way you survive
is no one else's damned business?

Kiss the Dread

And darling, I hope you remember:

To kiss the ghosts goodnight.
They are only older versions of you
that you have had to discard and forget.

And I have faith that when you put the sins to bed
you check under their beds for monsters,
just to say hello to them after all these years.

I hope you summon your courage
and you invite your demons to tea,
and you learn to listen to all their stories.

Sometimes war is not the answer.
After all, light needs the darkness
to glisten against, what are we without our sins?

The moon's glow in rhapsody calm
would hardly be so soothing without
the dark shawl night drapes behind it.

So sing a soft lullaby
to the things you hate about yourself,
and get to know them too.

Remind yourself the gentleness
of your own love is also meant to go
to the very darkest parts of you.

Four Spells to Keep Inside Your Mouth

'I respect myself' – the most powerful incantation that will change your whole life if you believe it when you say it.

'My heart is too valuable for you' – the spell that will set you free from any destructive soul.

'I believe in you' – the best gift you can ever give anyone else.

'No' – a single, commanding, two-letter spell with the ability to liberate you, if only you learn to use it unapologetically and cast it without fear.

Forest Person

When was the last time you spoke
to the trees that are growing inside
your mind, the leaves in your sinews?

When was the last time you fell
in love with the roots they leave
inside the base of you?

Did you not know
that you are where fairies roam?
That you are where the spirit bends?

You are already
simmering secrets sweet
to be savoured in silence,

just you and no one else.
Soft secrets like you are best
kept to yourself.

This world will lie to you
and tell you that forest inside you
does not exist.

Do not believe
the well-meaning words of people
who have not heard the birds inside you take flight.

Do not believe the hurtful words of people
who would prefer to turn you into a forest fire,
reduce you to soot and ash.

Do not believe anything
except the whispers
of the trees.

They have never
lied to you.
They won't start now.

The Healing

Sometimes healing
is the way you become yourself,
a path made of thorns
which could lead you
to your own incredible destiny.

Sometimes healing
is how Little Red Riding Hood
became the wolf,
because every woman
has a howl trapped in her chest.

Sometimes healing
is how Cinderella
never gave up on herself,
because she knew deep down
how to love herself.

Sometimes healing
is the story of a villainess
who was not a villainess at all,
just someone hurting from their trauma
and not having a good friend to call.

Sometimes healing
wears the name of a human
when you are stuck in a tower
with no other way down
but your own long hair.

But on most days healing
wears your own name
painted in your own blood,
messy, hard to tame,
but the only way to learn self-love.

Happily Ever After

I was never taught
graceful love until I met you
and found my heart in sync with yours.

You helped me build
a happily ever after and made me
believe in my own soul's core.

Thank you for opening
your souls to me, my sisters,
when all others were closed doors.

Thank you for loving me
when I still tasted
of heartache and war.

Acknowledgements

There are so many people I owe words of gratitude to that it would fill libraries if I wrote them down. What a blessing it is to live on this earth with so many people with such good hearts and thank you sometimes falls short.

So to start this, with heartfelt gratitude to: my parents and grandparents for giving me the gift of thousands of stories and thousands of books to read. My brother for always giving me perspective and supporting me. Emma for being the incredible and patient editor and wonderful friend that she is. Clare and my little Layla for being my family. Steve for standing by me even when I thought I was all alone. Bianca and Chris for always believing in me and the work. Tristan and Joanna for being the most excellent people with the biggest hearts. Amanda and Trista for being the soft, good souls that this universe has placed on this earth to show it what kindness is. Tomas, Anne, Zabiba, Leanne and all the lovely people at Trapeze who made this book a possibility. Shaun and Alison for being so welcoming and wonderful. Leopoldo for being my guardian angel. Emma and Lauz for their gentle spirits and warm laughter and love.

And finally, to you, dear reader, for seeing this journey with me through the magic and the fairytales and the legends to the end. I hope it aids you whilst you are out there building your own marvellous fairytale too.

About the Author

Nikita Gill is a British-Indian wri... ...the... south of England. With a huge pas... ...she... ...restaurants and minds all over...

Follow Nikita's work:
instagram: @nikita.gill
tumblr: meanwhilepoetry.tumblr.com
facebook: nikitagillwrites
twitter: @nktgill

About the Author

Nikita Gill is a British-Indian writer and poet living in the south of England. With a huge online following, she has entranced hearts and minds all over the world.

Follow Nikita's work:
Instagram: @nikita_gill
Tumblr: meanwhilepoetry.tumblr.com
Facebook: nikitagillwrites
Twitter: @nktgill